The Stairstep Girls: Images of Childhood

Written by Laura Compton
Edited by Donna Singleton

Copyright 2017 by Laura Compton. No part of this book may be used in any form or by any means graphical, electronic, or mechanical without written permission of the copyright owner.

ISBN: 978-1-987852-11-0

First printing June 2017

Publisher: Wood Island Prints; 670 Trans-Canada Highway, RR1; Belle River, PE C0A 1B0; (902) 962-3335; schultz@pei.sympatico.ca; www.woodislandsprints.com

Printing: Lightning Source Inc. (US); 1246 Heil Quaker Blvd, La Vergne, TN 37086; USA; (615) 213-5815 inquiry@lightningsource.com; www.lightningsource.com

Additional copies of this book may be obtained from the author, the editor or ordered through www.amazon.com

THE STAIR-STEP GIRLS

The hardest part of writing was untangling and rewriting the many memories jotted down at odd times through the day, on whatever scrap of paper was at hand. These images of childhood stand out so clearly even after so many years. It is dates which remain my downfall even as they were in school—especially history tests.

These accounts are all true events, written over the years as a form of amusement. Granted there were hard times in the depression days that were not amusing, but that is part of the past too—remembered but not dwelt on. I strongly believe that laughter is more healing to the soul than tears. May you who read my first attempt at memories in print find enjoyment from it as you also recall your own precious memories.

I begin with a brief history of our family to give you a picture of how our life was in the depression, and go on to later years in hopes of redeeming me somewhat from the antics of a young girl. Ours was a large family of thirteen with nine girls in a row (except for the second child a baby boy who died at three months—a brother we never knew). Coming about a year or so apart, we referred to ourselves as The Stair Step Girls. I was the fifth step.

Three brothers came at the end of our reign of girls. The first brother of the three was killed in an accident at the young age of twenty, leaving all who loved him sorrowing, but by then the two younger brothers were growing up and replaced us girls in the job of turning our poor parent's hair grey.

We lived in three different houses, each a little bigger than the last as our numbers increased. We always stayed in the Wood Islands area—the same district where I now live and will always call home.

1: Reflections

When starting this book of childhood, I intended to stop at what I imagined was adulthood and the years of marriage and raising my own family. But soon I realized that you never need to leave the joys of youth behind no matter how many years you have added to your frame. Little children will always bring out the child in you. You can still sit at the beach and help build sand castles; you can share their crayons, and make beautiful pictures even if it turns out to be a blue cat or a purple pig. Who could ever be too old to tumble around in soft fallen snow, hearing the delightful laughter of grandchildren? Could you be too old to help dress their dolls in clothes you have made from the scraps of material saved for years just for this purpose?

As today's younger generation reaches a stage of video games and movies, most of which you cannot understand or even pronounce, you try to watch and join in. Even though by now poor Gram feels quite ancient, she is still happy to be able to give them memories to be recalled in their adult life.

As I look back on good times and hard times, my memories of life are like a patch-work quilt. You look at the beautiful patches more often than the drab ones you would prefer to hide away in your memory closet. Nevertheless they are sewn together with the colourful ones to become the pattern of your life—who you are.

This little book is my quilt. The stitches may be uneven and the patches look worn as my aging memory fails.

The hard knocks of life can make you or break you—it's up to you.

When climbing up life's ladder and you take five steps up and fall down four, never give up. Step back and start over. You'll appreciate the view from the top for a job well done. Just a little bit of wisdom that comes with age!

2: Early Life at the Shore

My earliest memories are the days of living by the shore were the red clay and golden sand—our playground. A little fishing village of sorts with four or five little fishing boats tied out in the water and reached with a small dory. Grandpa Mosher owned a lobster factory to process the catch of the day. It was built out from the beach, supported on posts, and the fish, when cooked, was canned and sealed by hand with a torch and soldering iron. I don't imagine much was exported at that time although rules were very relaxed as to inspection of quality.

Images of my 'at shore grandparents' home come back as I write. A little glass vase embossed with red roses sits on a shelf above grandpa's big rocking chair, I see Gram's white wooden floors. They were made that way by daily scrubbings of white sand that we children, had to haul up in pails from the banks of the creek that ran out to the ocean. I went back many years later looking for that little creek and its banks of white sand, but as with all things of life it had eroded away with time.

As small children we were trusted to go shopping for essentials up at the little store in one part of our neighbour's house. I remember one particular trip with a list of: 1) cream of tartar 2) a bottle of kerosene oil, and 3) a fig of twist that resembled our now liquorice candy. Being young children, as we walked along, afraid of forgetting what we were sent for we made a singing rhyme of the items to be brought back home. This little tune went like this, "I got me cream of tartar, me tobaccy and me oil. We'll stir them all together and we'll put them on to boil." Unfortunately the 'tobaccy' didn't make it all the way home intact. Being inquisitive children we decided to have a chew. I guess we didn't pay much attention to the two stages for the use of this product. Chewing and spitting! For we chewed and swallowed, arriving home very sick, very green, and so our tobaccy rhyme was sung no more.

Grandpa was a boat builder; his boats were very small compared to the size of fishing boats today. One boat of his fleet, called Little Bo Beep, was our favourite, for it had a cabin and a tiny living quarter with bunks built up the sides. Sometimes they would take us grandchildren on a 'night over', tied up at the wharf about a mile from home just east of where the Wood Islands Lighthouse now stands. Not a great distance from home, but to us kids it was a big adventure just to leave the shore. There was nothing more peaceful than to be rocked asleep by gentle waves, watched over by two loving grandparents. A memory well cherished.

There weren't very many visits from the doctor in those days; Dr. Brehaut trips would be from his home in Murray River with his horse and sleigh in the winter, and his little black canvas topped wagon in summer. His pay was usually made by exchanging services for eggs, fish, or vegetables, depending on which the patient had the most of. One home visit resulted from a fall. Our humble abode by the shore contained two levels, the lower one for eating and reading, the top deck was the sleeping area, which was reached by a "straight up" stairs, somewhat like a built-in ladder. Being around four at this time and still quite clumsy, I tumbled down those stairs head first. In a few months that fall produced a turkey egg sized abscess which the usual home remedies weren't curing. After the doctor had lanced

2: Early Life at the Shore:

and bandaged it, I remember quite clearly to this day the silver nickel he placed in my hand for being a brave girl. A nickel in those days seemed such a fortune to me, and it may well have been the only nickel the dear doctor had in his pocket. I really was the envy of my sisters getting all the attention—and especially that silver nickel.

The second incident of doctoring involved the man who ran the first aid post and my other sister while we still living at our shore home. As was the custom in those days, when a fishing boat out-lived its prime, it was hauled up, tipped over onto buoys, and beached on higher ground—a perfect sliding place for us over its sides. We soon tired of the game and decided to tip it right-side up with the help of two neighbour boys who wanted to be the captains and we the crew. Being quite young in years but very determined, we didn't realize that there wasn't enough strength in five pairs of hands and that old boat only came up about six inches and down just as quickly—right down on my sister's hand, totally mangling the middle finger. After getting her free the boys had enough sense to take us all up to their father, (the home Doctor) at the first aid post and see if he could save the finger (and our hides). After washing off the finger and examining it, he reported the only remedy was to cut it off at the first knuckle using the chopping block out back! I guess he never heard such hollering and screaming from such a scared bunch. He changed his mind and bandaged it up as it was and sent us home with a warning that our parents were going to have to deal with this one. He must have been a pretty good doctor for it healed in time. To this day, though, her finger is still quite misshaped but workable.

Such was our life at the shore, where amusements were very limited by today's standards, excusing the little mischiefs we created that always seemed to land us in hot water with our elders. Maybe we didn't have all the luxuries of life but it made for good memories to be laughed over in later life as they were recounted at our family gatherings.

3: GRANDMA'S PLACE

When I was close to five years old I went to live with my grandparents in Glen William. No cars in those days, but my father did have a bicycle for long trips. Being too small to ride on the cross bar, he attached a small round tin washtub to the back carrier which became my back seat, as we set off for grandma's. It must have seemed to me that I was going a thousand miles from home. Those sixteen miles was not made any easier on rough clay roads and high hills that looked like mountains from my back seat in a tin tub. Finally we made it there—not quite what this child was used to.

This set of grandparents was so different from the loving ones I left behind at home. Maybe they were raised with the understanding that children should be seen and not heard—quite an awakening for me, after having three older sisters who, like me, were always ready for mischief. It didn't take too long for the sun porch at the front of the house to become my safe sanctuary. It had a settee and pots and pots of geraniums on every window sill.

The old Eaton's catalogue was to become my story book, but oh what a story book! With pictures of such strange things, like a washing machine that didn't even resemble a wash tub, and radios you could plug into a wall. Beautiful dresses, shoes, and boots that weren't made of rubber like the war time gum rubbers we had to wear. "Rich folk's fancy things," Gram used to say. She didn't have electricity either. Oh, but the dolls with the beautiful little dresses and shoes were my favourite pages in my story book! How they passed my lonely days.

Grandfather was a very strict man with very little to say, he didn't have to I guess. One look when you were out of line was enough to send everyone scurrying out of sight, especially me. I do remember he had a little shop—a grocery store of sorts—on the other side of the apple orchard. I can only remember being in it one time when my Uncle Eddy, who was old enough, he thought, to go to a dance but didn't have enough change for admission, convinced me to be his lookout at the shop door while Grandpa was over at the house for dinner. Eddy's catch, about fifteen cents, my reward a chocolate bar from the shelf. It sure was a sweet treat for a little girl who didn't have any idea of what stealing meant. I still can't recall if Grandpa ever found out. I'm sure that I would have remembered if he did!

Grandma Acorn always made me nice little coats and dresses to wear—dresses made from my aunt's discarded ones. She would sit at her sewing machine in her bedroom and let me watch. That old peddle-machine fascinated me so much. If you can believe it, today I have a similar one on which I do all my sewing.

One little dress stands out most clearly in my mind—white with yellow flowers. They raised cattle for their milk and butter. The cattle were housed in an old red barn, away from the north side of the house, just down the hill from our little school up on the hill. Behind this barn ran a drain that carried awful liquids from the cattle inside. Guess who took a shortcut to school dressed in her little white dress? Little legs can't jump too far and didn't make it all the way over the drain. Running back into the house, the legs were washed off but the dress stayed on, splatters included, with a sermon from Grandma, "Land-a-mercy child, how can you be so clumsy? Now you march right back to school." I never

3: Grandma's Place: 13

questioned, I just did, but that little white dress with the yellow flowers is not one of my fondest memories.

Everyone on that farm had chores to do. My jobs were picking apples, climbing trees for cherries, and packing firewood in a little green building. I really didn't mind; sometimes it was fun and passed the long days.

Grandmother's house always seemed to be filled with adults—aunts and uncles all with large families as well, but all quite grown up so there were never any little children to play with.

That is until my dear Madeline who had recently married my Uncle Nathan came home for a summer visit. What a free spirit, I adored her, we went everywhere together. She became my playmate, exploring around the dam, picking wild flowers as we put the cows out to pasture. Fishing in the little brook at the bottom of the hill—we equipped ourselves with a broken branch, a piece of string, and a safety pin for a hook. How I missed her when she went home to Cape Breton. Even now sixty-five years later when we call each other on New Year's Eve we reminisce and laugh over our fishing trip with no fish.

Don't get me wrong. I believe Grandma, though very strict and maybe just a little tired with her own burdens, loved me in her own way. For when the corn would be all picked from the garden she would save me the silk tassels, give me a ball of yarn from which I could tie bunches together for the head, arms and legs of a corn silk doll. I sure must have loved it—I can still picture it in my mind.

I lived with my grandparents until sometime in my seventh year. When I found out that dearest Grandpa in Wood Islands was very ill, I just wanted to go home. I was put on a train in Murray River and was met by someone in a horse and sleigh. I don't remember who, but I do remember pulling off those awful red woollen stockings my gram made me wear, regardless of it being winter and lots of snow; sorry Gram!

I did get to see Grandpa Mosher before he died, I loved him dearly. I'll never forget that little black wagon hearse as it drove up to the door and took our beloved grandfather away, but we still had a very lively Gram, who proved to be a very interesting companion in the coming years and I was back home with my sisters once again. I could be as noisy and mischievous as the rest of them, so one chapter of life ended, and another one began.

4: WHITE MOLLY

I imagine in the period of any child's young life they owned a pet of some kind. Mine was White Molly, a beautiful fluffy ball of fur that later grew into a troublesome, wandering animal with a mind of her own. Almost weekly that white cat would go missing resulting in a search by every child in the house, amid sniffles and long calls of despair. Even our father, who considered them useless animals and actually didn't have any use for cats of any colour, often joined in the search. I sometimes wondered if he took a different path just to get away from his howling brood.

In those days the horse and wagon or sleigh was our only means of travel, and a cold means it was in the winter. Our little corner store carried mostly grocery supplies. If a larger item such as a new stove was needed, it required a trip to Montague, some twenty miles away. A few minutes' drive today, took the greater part of the day with a horse and sleigh. As was the custom, the men took along a little green 'teddy bottle', whose contents kept the blood warm and the bones from freezing. A weak excuse, but one often used on such trips. My father, was well warmed up when he reached Montague. As he was about to cross the bridge, what should be about to cross over too but a white cat which, in my father's state, looked like White Molly. So started the chase—leaving the horse and sleigh, he ran over the bridge calling, "Here Molly; here Molly." Quite an amusing sight to all who watched this spectacle. But not so to one particular person—the town's policeman. In those day's there couldn't have been any jails, for he placed my father in the cold storage plant at the end of the bridge, somewhere near where the museum now stands. There he stayed for a few hours until the effects of that little 'green teddy' wore off. After that incident, we girls and White Molly knew enough to stay out of sight and avoid mention of 'green teddies', white cats, or cold storage for quite some time. Our father, quite unlike us, could never see the humour of it at all!

5: Neighbours

With the onset of television, neighbourhood visiting changed forever. There were about seven families on our road and most had children, so we were never bored for something to do. As a child you could always spend your free time with the neighbour children, who were within walking distance of your home.

A widow with a young family of four around our ages was one of our favourite gathering places. She became our second Mom and had so much patience with us all, especially on rainy days when the boisterous gang of seven or eight children would be playing hide and seek all through her house. I cannot recall one cross word ever spoken from her. We played such funny little games in our youth with her children. When we played too long and darkness was coming we would say, "If you walk me halfway home, I'll walk you halfway back. Which by this time, after a few back and forth trips and growing quite dark, we relied on a grown up from either home to make the double trip to get each set of not-so-brave children safely home.

Between our home and this neighbour lived our school teacher, a very strict widow woman who was very dedicated to her job of educating us all. I'm sure she kept a vigil at her window to catch us goofing off instead of at home doing our everlasting homework. Many a time she would catch us as we went by her place and sent us back home with a lecture. Before long we became wise to her ways and crossed over in the woods in back of her house, quite unseen and very pleased with ourselves.

Even those who didn't have children always made us feel welcome. Our next door neighbours to the east were an elderly couple, who ran a small farm of one cow and some chickens. They always got us over at potato digging time. Their only means of digging was a few hoes and the big round baskets, which was our job to fill. Their old brown dog, Bob, must have thought he was one of the gang for he always wanted to help drag the big potato baskets down each row. It was such a nice place for a child to visit, and after a lesson on the Golden Rules of Life, we would always be treated to a lunch of biscuits, jam and a big glass of milk rich with cream. Making cream was another chore I enjoyed helping with (or what I thought at the time was helping), for I would turn and turn the handle of the cream separator for an hour—a chore that might have taken her half the time. The best part of this morning task was when I took each part of the separator apart to be washed and sterilized in hot water since each part still had a covering of rich cream which I could scrape off and enjoy (which in turn made my small frame grow very chubby). How that dear couple never tired of us, I'll never know for there was always one of us on their doorstep.

One old couple, well on in years lived quite close. He was a retired school teacher and sure looked the part, with his little round glasses perched on his sharp nose and his very stern stare as he quizzed us on history and geography. I admit I was just a little scared of him but I always kept going back. His wife, a sweet old lady who was very thin, always seemed to be clad in the same long grey dress and white apron with oversized pockets. How I eyed those big pockets to see if they held our surprise. She always waited until we were on our way out (and maybe out of sight of her stern

5: Neighbours:

husband) before she slyly handed us our treat. Maybe a little wrapped parcel or a pair of mittens with a dime or a nickel hidden in the thumb.

Our neighbours to the west had a family of three girls who shared in our childhood years. Their parents, who had orchards of many varieties of apples, kept us well supplied with summer fruit. But some apples, I must confess, were gotten on our apple raids. As children we liked the excitement of climbing well up in the branches where the ripest fruit were beyond our reach. Hoping to fill our pockets before being discovered by the owner, (who I often suspected liked the game of catch the thief). He always gave chase, but never a lecture.

The last family of four girls lived at the end of the row of houses on our road. Like me, the youngest was in her teen years and liked to go hiking after dark. Back then you could do so without fear of man or beast—with the exception of one mean old ram who acted as a watchdog for their farm and for some reason didn't like me any more than I liked him. He would wait in hiding, whenever I entered their yard after dark, sneak up behind me and, with a good bunt on my rear, send me sailing in the air. No matter how many times this went on neither one would give up trying to outsmart the other.

Our little community was like one big family of caring and sharing for each other. The majority of children were also girls, with the exception of two young boys, who were brought up by their single-parent mothers. They were both very quiet young lads, so the burden of initiating mischievous pranks was left to the dozen or so female tots and teens of Grey's Road.

As I write so many years later, maybe some reader who lived the same lean years of the thirties and forties as we did will share with me the antics and memories of my childhood and look back on their own with the same amusement.

6: The Train

Can you recall the long, lonesome, haunting sound of the train whistle as it passed through our many districts and stopped at each station along the way? The mail arrived by rail and was taken by the carrier to each post office and delivered to each household by horse and sleigh or wagon depending on the season. The station and little store were close by and it was a favourite gathering place for older gents and young teens. Both curious no doubt for news about the outside world from returning passengers or maybe just as an excuse to pass a long evening.

The trip to Charlottetown was quite an excursion. You left the station around seven in the morning and got back sometime in the later evening, depending on weather conditions. The trip seemed the longest, especially the loop at Lake Verde, where you travelled for hours. It seemed to circle the other stations along the line and end up at the very same station you started from. While the train had a three-hour stopover, you rushed uptown to do your business or shopping. I'm sure our shopping was very limited and rarely done for it took a lot of penny saving just for the ticket. Most times we went just for the fun of the ride.

The trip home in winter was the one we enjoyed the most, with the warmth of the little coal burning stove at the end of the passenger car. It took me quite a while to figure out why some of the male passengers seemed in such a merry mood on the way home. I remember the music of the guitar and accordion as the merrier got merrier and it wasn't very long before everyone joined in on the singing. A few more hours, a few more miles until reality and tomorrow's work.

While riding the train home, if you saw a group of old timers huddled around one seat, you knew a good yarn was in progress—not suitable no doubt for the ears of young ladies and girls.

One particular joke was a favourite. The conductor would go back and forth calling each station coming up. As he was passing an old farmer, he kept chanting, "Iona Station, Iona Station." To which the old gent said, "Don't know what in the devil you're bragging about, I own a whole dang farm of fifty acres."

The train wasn't just for transporting passengers; it consisted of many box cars, which were loaded with pulp and lumber—the main export at the time. The railroad also employed men to unload coal at each station to run the engines. Many times at unloading time, coal that was left on the ground was taken home in potato sacks to keep home fires burning. I remember how I hated that oily smell of burning coal and the black soot it left on your hands. Train service terminated in 1986, taking away with it a way of country life replaced by truck and automobile. Gone are the sound of the lonesome whistle, the clickity-clack of iron wheels on steel, and the trail of black smoke lingering in the air. Simple little things future generations will never experience again on PEI.

7: Foods and Fashions

The lean times of the depression pretty well dictated the foods available for the dinner table. But you could always depend on a belly full of homemade bread and beans. I wonder what my mom would think of those new electric bread makers that pop out one loaf a day—her daily batch consisted of at least twelve loaves and once a week, if raisins were available, the same number of loaves of raisin bread, as only Mom could make them. Although I've made many hundreds of loaves of bread during my lifetime, I was never able to get one that equalled hers. I can never remember Mom having a cookbook, maybe that was her secret; whatever she had the most of went into her baking. As I remember Mom's bread I can just picture one little modern electric loaf in the middle of our dinner table, surrounded by a husband, wife, and brood of hungry kids. It would be like throwing one small sardine to a bunch of starving cats. I'm pretty sure that's what you would call a real howling cat fight.

During the war years sugar and butter were household commodities that were hoarded and doled out sparingly, much like a miser protecting his treasured wealth. When the allotted ration coupons for the week were used, there was no way to get more even if you had the money. The only alternative was if you could trade unused gas or butter coupons with a neighbour who might have an extra sugar stamp.

For some reason there was always a good supply of black strap molasses and beans, two food staples not suitable for export overseas. If you had a big meal of those two you would understand why molasses could always be counted on for a good laxative and beans, well we all know the after effects of this food! Not a very good combination to feed soldiers at war, especially those held up for hours in a trench or dugout. A much better food for those folks back home living with the wide open spaces of farm and field!

Potatoes were always available and filled many a rumbling tummy. This food could be prepared in many ways. It could be boiled in skins and served with salt herring—the blue potato was best for this. Salt cod was best served with white potatoes, with the leftovers made into fishcakes or hash—usually for the supper. Boiled, mashed or fried, the potato was the king of the table.

French fries were quite different from those now served worldwide. A big round sliced potato, fried golden brown in a pan of hardened pork fat and a side dish of bread and molasses. Ketchup may have been around at this time but not for us.

In the hardest of times 'stone soup' could always be a standby for a belly filler, although not exactly the most gourmet of foods. According to the legend this soup originated when an old farmer got tired of his cook complaining that there was no meat for her pot, and so told her to throw in a stone. Lord knows he had enough of them on his farm. The legend had others coming along and adding bits until a real soup resulted. In practice it was very easy to make, even for young girls. A dozen or so sliced potatoes, half a pot of boiling water, two large onions, half a cup of pork drippings and seasoned with salt and pepper, sapped up with a chunk of homemade bread. Years later when Campbell's came out with tomato soup in a can, adding it to stone soup and produced 'tomato potatoes'—a soup my kids still like and ask

7: Foods and Fashions : 25

me to make.

Another war-time food that graced many a supper table was the big pilot-saucer-sized cracker or hard tacks. The good ones were sent overseas to the soldiers but the broken ones were sold to the local grocery store. For a few cents you could get a big brown paper bag full. Heaped on a dinner plate and dribbled all over with molasses, it was enough to hold you over until the next morning—everlasting porridge.

There were few if any packaged foods in our young days. You took your brown gallon jar to the store to be pumped full of molasses; the same with your jar for kerosene oil for your lamps. Other supplies went into brown bags from the many wooden bins of beans, sugars, oatmeal and other necessities of daily living.

Flour was always in cotton sacks with the bright dyed image of Robin Hood. At home with thorough bleaching those sacks were recycled into pillow cases and string tied bloomers. Many a young lass, bending over, flashed a faded image of Robin Hood or worse yet, when the string became undone there it was around your ankles.

Grocery shopping was a chore usually left to the older children. There was always hope the old store keeper would be in a good mood and give you a free stick of penny candy for your trudge home, all loaded with gallon jars and many brown bags of supplies. Lord forgive us if they got mixed together or the ends came out of the bags and they didn't make it all the way home.

How very different was our young life to those of today. No treat's, no menu's, you gave thanks and ate all that was placed in front of you and if you didn't, no doubt it would wind up as your supper.

The war put many restrictions on daily life in both

city and country. Everyone did what they could for the cause and knew whatever they had to sacrifice was nothing compared to what our young soldiers had to live through. Even though we lived so far from the battlefields, I can recall being scared when we had blackouts. Every window must be covered and we could never understand how the enemy could see our little oil lamp from his plane so high in the sky. The thing I feared most was when the warning siren would wail and the search lights in town would criss-cross all over the night sky. As children we would tremble when the talk of war came over our battery radio—everyone sat in hushed silence to hear the voice of doom barely audible over the crackling static. As I grew older my heart pained for those children of the foreign countries who had to live through the real thing, real bombs!

People became very imaginative and inventive, when it came to making substitutes for the many things they had known before the war. Coveralls replaced fancy dresses and skirts of career fashion, as many worked in factories making war supplies.

Nylon stockings, which no well-clad lass would be without, were no longer available, as all nylon was diverted to parachutes. Some creative person—a woman no doubt—invented a paste much like liquid make up of today which one applied to the legs from the toe to the thigh. When dried it would be marked down the back with a fine black liner to resemble the seam which was quite fashionable as the glamour legs of this period! It worked quite well in dry weather but not so well if your date wanted to go for a stroll on a damp evening. Your beautiful legs gradually produced a light brown puddle seeping through your open-toed shoes or high heeled sandals. Believe me from experience it could be very embarrassing. Thank Heaven for the invention of panty hose—one quick pull on and you're on your way!

8: Working Days

Mom and Dad were both very hard workers. They took jobs no matter how hard, to provide for their family. Mostly pulp cutting was with a buck saw or axe, for those were before the chain saw, (or at least I don't ever recall them having one), nor did they own a tractor. Many a time they would carry the cut pulp out on their shoulders to be stacked by the side of the road. This was the period in our lives when family farming was ending with the selling or trading of our horses for something more essential, such as food. There were times Mom and Dad had to stay in a camp that was close to the woodlot, for the distance was too far for daily travel. They had no choice but to rely on the older children to stay at home and care for the smaller ones, while they were gone through the week of work at the camp.

We learned responsibility at an early age. I guess it was thought if you were old enough to prepare meals you were old enough to work for them and we all had our turn. At the age of twelve my turn came—the days of being in charge weren't too bad, but the nights were long and lonely and the responsibility of it all seemed too much. I remember one night when it was my turn to be the head of the house, a terrible thunder storm was raging. The little ones were all asleep in their beds and I was scared. "Oh Lord," I said to myself, "How do I handle this one?" I guess my words to myself reached the ears of Someone else and became a prayer, which was heard. I gathered all the little ones up from their sleep, piled them in Mom and Dad's big bed and

8: Working Days:

sang every hymn I knew until the storm passed.

Being a substitute mother at such an early age really makes you grow up fast. I often wondered in later life how Mom ever coped with it all and still stayed so cheerful after working hard all day and then coping with her female brood.

Pulp cutting wasn't easy on clothing, which at the best of times was scarce. Many evenings I watched Mom patch overalls that were past redemption, having more holes in them than a hundred-year-old tin bucket. Patch was sewn over patch and all by hand to get by for a little while longer. Like so many other mothers of that age, she had her own inventive way of making each thing last just a little longer. When woollen mitts were still useable, except for the worn out palms, she would cut out a shape from the legs of worn out coveralls and stitch it to the front of the mitt. Thus making do with the hope that Christmas would bring a new pair.

The saying, "a woman's work is never done," must have been meant for our mom, for her work days were long and hard—no electricity, no push button washing machine, or anything compared to the easy life of today. She had just her two small hands and an old kitchen stove that cooked so many meals, usually heated with green wood which was sometimes dug out from under a pile of snow in winter.

As I write and recall her life as a young mother, I wonder if we as children realized all that she did, all that she gave. Those were hard times in the forties when as the saying goes, you got through each day by the skin of your teeth, hoping tomorrow would be better.

9: Old Tangle Foot and Jack

I'm sure there came a time in every farmer's life in the forties, when one of his horses out-lived their working days. Rather than feeding them, they were sold or traded for something more useful to the farmer.

Horse trading was somewhat of a sport. Through one trade we became the owner of an old grey mare that closely resembled an old camel, with the hump turned inward, that left such a hollow a saddle wasn't needed. Besides the ungainly appearance, Old Grey had another disadvantage; one of her front legs was gnarled and crooked. Thus arose the name Old Tangle Foot.

When I was around nine or ten the old gal and I sort of adopted each other. I became her chosen bare-back rider, with a harness made from an old patched halter and a few feet of rope. In those days my father had a job loading pulp into boxcars at the Wood Islands train station. As was the custom he carried his noon lunch in a tin pail. One day in late spring he had set off for work minus his lunch. I don't recall the reason, but more than likely the bread bin was empty and the new batch not yet cooked. Old Tangle Foot and I were elected to take the path through the woods and deliver his lunch at noon. Picture in your mind a little girl riding bare back on this sad looking horse with the tin lunch pail dangling at the end of the rope reigns.

Halfway through the path Old Tangle Foot, being quite old and tired, took his usual stumble, landing belly up in the mud. The girl and the pail didn't fair of much better,

9: Old Tangle Foot and Jack: 31

for when Old Grey rolled, so did the lunch, right under the old humped back. After we managed to both get upright, I took stock of the mess we were in. Oh boy, what a mess! I knew my father, who had been loading since early dawn, would be both starving and angry by then, waiting for his dinner. Our gentle Mom had promised hot bread and molasses. I just didn't know in which direction to go. Deliver the lunch, which by now resembled a motile pancake of hot bread and molasses, topped off with grey horse hair. I must have chosen the latter option—head off for safety and Mom, for I lived to see another day. No doubt Old Tangle Foot and I got into more scrapes while she lived. I loved and trusted her, her slow gate and those bony ribs made such a good place to practice your counting.

    Our father must have been quite a horse trader in those days. I recall another old recycled black stallion named Jack. Jack had the idea that he had the right of way even in winter when roads were rerouted to one lane going through the neighbouring fields where the snow wasn't as deep. One winter day, Dad, my sisters, and I decided to go to Murray River. We hitched Jack to the sleigh and away we went. All went well until we met our old mailman coming up in the opposite direction in this one lane track. Old Jack decided then and there, as did the mailman that he was coming through. I can still see that old guy with the box of his sleigh tipped upright, covering his angry face like a picture frame—much like the angry face of our father when he was told to keep that dang crazy horse and those dang crazy girls off the road.

    Another trait of Old Jack's was when he wanted a drink he was going to get a drink, no matter what—even if the stream was at bottom of a hill away from the road. Down he goes, breaking the sleigh from its harness, getting all the water he wanted and then dragging three frightened riders—still clutching the reigns—back to the road.

Although there were many other horses in our young lifetime, those are the last two I remember. Maybe by this time our father decided that horses had to go and traded them, no doubt, for the old truck which the girls were forbidden to lay their hands on. Must have worked for I don't remember ever getting behind the wheel.

10: Halloween

Halloween in the forties was a time of great planning to come up with better tricks than the ones you did in the past years. The usual ones included raiding apple orchards, hoping the owners would be on guard to give us a good chase, or tipping over the old wooden toilets, but as we got into our teen years tricks became pranks. Four stand out in my memory. I guess it is safe to confess all now, fifty plus years later.

The devil's screech, was a good one. A most horrible sound could be made when a long piece of thread was attached to a nail on the outside window and rubbed back and forth with a piece of yellow rosin, snatched from a fiddle case—usually Uncle Harry's, who was quite the fiddler at this time. I wonder how many times we scared the devil out of someone before we were caught. That awful sound would vibrate all through the house, Uncle's included. He hated Halloween and became our main target.

We dreamed up lots of pranks including another one which involved our own father. At the time he owned a little old truck—a Model A or T, which quite resembled Jed Clampett's on the Beverly Hillbillies Show. It being Halloween and afraid some of these young ruffians would harm it, he pulled up a chair by the window in full view of his prized possession, intending to keep a long night's vigil. Of course being a part of these young ruffians, we girls knew of his plans and spread the word. My father had been working in the woods since dawn and by this time was all tuckered out.

He closed his eyes and slept like a baby—still in his chair and still keeping watch. This was what we were all waiting for. Away went the little old truck rolling down the hill, across the road into a field, hid in a clump of bushes, undamaged and quite invisible, except for those wooden racks. We snuck back home and got into bed before he woke up.

I'm sure we scouted all year for our next plan. This time it was an old cement mixer—a contraption that looked like a monster iron butter churn, with a handle on one side to pull back and forth to mix up the contents inside. There it sat back of the barn right next to the manure pile. You guessed it, into that mixer goes the soft mushy manure. I bet that old farmer cursed Halloween and those awful teens.

Prank number four required a bigger gang, more muscle and lots of rope. Two neighbours who lived side by side at this time were feuding and wouldn't speak to each other. One owned a two wheeled dump cart and the other a barn down a little piece from each farm. Maybe the only time we were quiet that night was when we were hauling that old cart down to the barn. With half the gang on each side of the barn we pulled on that rope, one side up; one side down; until that old two wheeler sat straddled over the roof, one wheel on each side. I don't recall how long it stayed there or which farmer gave in first and took it down. Sometimes even now when driving through town and seeing the old cars used for advertisement perched on the dealer's roof, it reminds me of that last Halloween we spent as teens. I guess we were finally growing up.

11: Home Remedies

Most country people rarely called on a doctor except in severe emergencies, instead relying on the home remedies that were handed down from generation to generation—vile tasting concoctions of herbs and minerals readily available around the farm, which did have a healing effect for most minor ailments.

The best known home remedy was the mustard plaster, a mixture of flour, mustard, and water, spread between two layers of flannel and placed on the chest to cure minor cases of pneumonia or pleurisy. I don't know the benefits the flour, but that hot mustard sure burned the bedevil out of your soul.

Spring time tonics were the worst remedy of all. The whole body had to be purged from all those long winter imperfections with a cream made from soft lard and sulphur which was worked into the skin. You were well into the hot days of summer before your body stopped emitting an odour much like that of the pulp mill that drifted across the strait on a rainy day with a south-east wind.

The ointment for most burns and one that I can attest to for home healing was the oil or grease from the Christmas goose. It was strained and stored in a glass jar. At a young age, as I rocked in my little chair, I toppled head first onto the hot parlour stove which left my face a mass of blisters. Dear Gram, who was living with us at this time, covered me good with that well preserved goose grease. It left me smelling like one of the barn yard flock but it worked like magic, leaving not so much as a little scar.

A few over-the-counter medications were available at the corner store, my favourite being niture, which came in a little brown bottle and was mixed with hot water and a good helping of sugar. It was the sweetest of cold remedies, much like the hot toddies for the grownups, but you sure did get a good night's sleep. I believe it contained sixty percent alcohol and forty percent medicine.

A sore throat was treated with hot camphorated-oil, rubbed into the neck, and then wrapped with a warm woollen sock. The odour of the sock was disguised by the pungent fumes of hot camphor, which also cleared up a stuffy nose.

Boils were quite common from farm labour and fishing and everyone had their favourite poultice. Yellow Sunlight Soap mixed with white sugar was the most popular one, but some swore by a mixture of bread and onion boiled in hot milk.

The most frowned upon remedy for an earache was for an adult to blow smoke from the corn cob pipe into the affected ear and seal it off with a wad of cotton batting. Seems quite an unusual cure but it always stopped an earache and never affected our hearing.

Can anyone ever forget the childhood medicines of pure cod-liver-oil and castor oil? The first one had the picture of a cod fish on the label with the taste and smell of one being well decomposed, leaving you burping for days with the taste. The second wasn't much better. If you didn't run fast enough, your parent would catch you, and hold your nose and make you swallow. The rest of the day was spent in the outhouse with the Eaton's catalogue.

I'm sure Gram Mosher was the inventor of home remedies and we children were her not-so-willing subjects.

11: Home Remedies:

She made the vilest tasting concoctions to cure every ailment, including her boiled tansy leaves to purify the blood in spring, and others to horrible to mention. She was a firm believer in the healing power of Mother Nature, be it animal, vegetable or mineral.

As a young child I went out fishing with my father and slipped driving the gaff (a curved hook on a pole for catching buoy's) right into the middle of my knee cap. When they carried me home and laid me down, Dear Gram poured a few drops of turpentine right into the wound. Now that's pain! However, I recovered without a trace of infection from the dirty hook. I have no doubt all her other cures worked just as well. I have often wondered how we as children survived, for the cures were often worse than the disease.

Children were usually born at home with the help of a midwife but a call was made to the doctor in case of any emergency. Usually by the time he arrived there was another addition to the family and nothing for him to do but have a quick hot-toddy and be on his way.

Such was our health care in the past, but our bodies were healthier in the days of our not so modern world thanks to pure air, and a land and sea free of chemicals

12: The Kitchen Party

Most everyone could come up with a reason to hold a home party after a hard week of work. Saturday and Sunday were time off. Weekends were the usual time for weddings. Most young couples had their wedding feasts at their own dining room table, joined by every relative known, young and old, which made for a lively time in most small homes. If there wasn't a wedding or such to celebrate, someone always came up with a good excuse to whoop it up on a Saturday night. As was the custom when the feasting was over and all cleared away, out came the little teddy bottles of green, filled with homemade liquid refreshment. Tired bodies and sore muscles were soon forgotten and everyone took their turn at step dancing on the bare kitchen floor, accompanied by the toe tapping music of the fiddler, mouth organ, and if someone in the group was talented enough to handle them, the spoons. Odd times or should I say most of the time after too much male boasting as to who was the stronger or just too much of the night's refreshments, things would end up in an outdoor free for all. This always amused the little heads stuck out of the open upstairs window after being sent to bed.

13: HOME GROWN; HOMEMADE

Once discarded, everything around the home could be brought back and made useful again. An old engine bonnet made a perfect toboggan for coasting. When an old molasses puncheon (or barrel as it would be called now) was torn apart the curved staves that made up the sides could be made into a pair of skis of sorts, with pieces of rope for binding tied over the boots. They sure produced strong leg muscles, for the only way to make them shiny and smooth was a few good trips over the hard snow packed hill.

When you sawed off the end of a birch or maple log you had cart wheels to attach with spikes to an old wooden crate, making a most useful wagon for hauling firewood.

A slingshot was made from a Y shaped branch with a rubber band pulled back for aim. A boy's toy, but then there were no boys in our early family, only tomboys as rough and tumble girls were called. Those slingshots were very destructive to glass windows and exposed parts of the body made a perfect target.

An old red cutter sleigh with curved half rounded runners still intact but shafts and other parts missing served once again as a coasting sled. That is until the time we decided to take Gram with us on an evening run. Living at the top of the hill we could get a good fast start. In first went Gram, but that old sleigh just didn't wait for the rest of us to hop in. The ground was hard and crusty from the freezing rain upon white snow and away she went down the hill, across the road, into the next field where she was finally stopped, thank heavens, by a snow bank, soft and protected by a clump of alder bushes. Dear Gram forgave us much sooner it seemed than our parents. The list of things good girls don't do became even longer with that old sleigh topping the list. I'm sure before they got us all grown up there would be more additions.

It seemed everything on the farm was homemade or home grown. Animals were raised and butchered when the first good frost set in which was our form of a freezer. I remember our father would go out to the barn with a long carving knife and cut of slivers of frozen meat for each day's meals. No part of an animal was ever wasted. Ham and bacon were cured with a pink smoky smelling powder which often reminded me of kindling drying in the hot oven. The innards were thoroughly washed out and stuffed with a mixture of ground meat. Parts of the head were boiled with other ingredients to make pans and pans of potted meat which was set out in the frost to gel.

The chickens and geese also produced many a meal, especially at Christmas. I'm reminded of our cocky little bantam rooster who was included in the flock. As with most folk, at the time of Christmas preparations a pile of mash was left over after the distilling of the Holiday Cheer. Old bantam thought it was his food, and consumed a little too much. He hopped and danced across the yard as if he were listening to a fiddle tune of The Chicken Reel. I don't know if we ever got that cocky little thing sober enough to throw into the boiling pot.

Christmas stockings were very different than those of today. Store-bought toys were a luxury we never knew. We got an orange scribbler, a pencil, and one little strip of ribbon candy which we stretched out for many days. Its sweet memory would have to last until the next days of Santa. In one more abundant year I got a real store-bought toy in my sock—a little broom just my size with a skinny red handle.

When reminiscing about Christmas past with my younger sisters, the gifts they remembered most were the rag dolls I made each of them. At a young age I loved to work with needle and thread. Maybe, being older, I knew the disappointment of a stocking and no doll. They said they treasured those little dolls with head and face made from a ball of nylons, painted features of crayons, yarn hair, dresses from scraps covering their long dangling limbs made from strips of old sock tops—the only part left useable. We may not have been rich, but we were happy and treasured each gift given, knowing the sacrifice of our parents when times were quite lean in our large family.

14: Hired Out

Work for pay was very hard to come by in the mid-thirties. Most males of the family went away to search for jobs. The logging camps of New Brunswick seemed the most logical place, as lumber was in great demand, which left the grandparents and wives to carry on back home.

When you were old enough to go out working, young people in their teens were hired out. The boys often went to neighbouring districts as farm hands and the young girls were taken on as maids. Most of those jobs were when school was out for the summer. 'Allowance' was an unknown word in those days. What little you earned went into the family pot and you never questioned, you just did.

My two sisters were hired as maids and when it came my turn, age fourteen and quite small in stature like my mother, I sure wasn't ready for the task that lay ahead of me. Instead of singing for our supper we had to work for it.

My first job as a hired maid was just a few miles from home, but it was a very lonesome time for me. Having to start work so early in the morning, I had to live in with the family. The family I worked for consisted of a husband, wife, their young son, their brother-in-law, and a bedridden old aunt who needed daily care. This part of my duties I did not mind, for she was a sweet old lady. I would spend many hours in the evenings reading to her instead of the lonely times after dark that I would have had to spend in my little room up the back stairs—maid quarters, as they were called in country homes—clean and neat but no frills. Being very shy in those days, the little room and my books were my comfort until morning.

Electricity wasn't available in most country areas and the daily washing depended on the day's weather. This chore was the hardest part of my service for it was done outside on a platform close to the pump and clothesline. Being so small, I also needed a scrubbing board. There always seemed to be mounds and mounds of white sheets that had to be washed, rinsed and wrung out by hand. I don't know which were the worse, those sheets or the farm work clothes that required a lot of scrubbing with homemade lye soap. The results of this were very red hands and scraped knuckles.

The tending of the cattle and milking was not part of your contract but it usually became so if the crops had to be tended to at this time and extra hands were needed.

Regardless of your age, your workday started at dawn and ended at dusk after the evening meal was over and washing up was done. Twelve hours of work for fifty cents was the standard wage for a maid, or five cents an hour adding up to fifteen dollars a month for a job well done and a little more food on your family's table. A hard life, yes, but it made you appreciate the better times that came later.

My next employment came after I completed schooling at fifteen. This job was so different! As a factory worker I guess I was considered an adult. At least the pay check was all mine, to do with as I wished, and I did—all $36.25 for two weeks of work.

I shall never forget my first ever new outfit—a blue taffeta dress that swished with a rustling sound of wealth and black baby-doll shoes. Feeling much like Cinderella, I went to my first adult dance and left childhood behind. At seventeen I married and started my own family of five, each with their own original antics to relate to their children and not copying, I hope, those of their Mother.

Here I end my journal. My life has had many chapters, each with its own memories—each one an image as vivid as if the events were yesterday and not 66 years ago when my childhood as I remember it, began. With this I would like to leave with you a little piece of poetry of mine set in those leaner years.

14: Hired Out:
The Helping Hand

By the sweat of their brow, in the hot blazing sun
They tilled the rough land, till the harvest was done.
The toil it was great; the days they were so long.
A two handled plough, and his work team so strong.
He questioned not the difficult life that he led
Was a labour of love to ensure his family was fed.
He laboured not alone when harvest time drew near.
For the onset of white frost was each farmer's great fear.
For neighbour helped neighbour with no thought of pay.
Just a favour returned with his crops put away.
Hard-working people who had pride in their land.
Supporting each other with respect and an outstretched hand.
Tired muscles renewed at a dinner of the most
                                                   wholesome fare
Prepared by farm women who had all gathered there.
Steaming bowls of potatoes, and a home cured baked ham
Topped off with a large helping of gooseberry jam.
I ponder of the future and what the changes will bring.
Will they remember their customs or will the dollar be king?
For time passes so quickly in this new modern age.
Will their lives be recorded or forgotten on some
                                                   yellowing page?

By Laura Compton

www.ingramcontent.com/pod-product-compliance
Lightning Source LLC
Chambersburg PA
CBHW030534080526
44586CB00011B/432